VOLVER EN TINTA
REBORN IN INK

Reborn in Ink

LAURA CESARCO EGLIN

Translated by Jesse Lee Kercheval
and Catherine Jagoe

INTERNATIONAL EDITIONS
Barbara Goldberg, Series Editor

THE WORD WORKS
WASHINGTON, D.C.

Reborn in Ink © 2019 Jesse Lee Kercheval & Catherine Jagoe

Reproduction
of any part of this book
in any form or by any means,
electronic or mechanical,
except when quoted
in part for the
purpose
of review,
must be with
permission in writing
from the publisher.

Address inquiries to:
The Word Works
P.O. Box 42164
Washington, D.C. 20015
editor@wordworksbooks.org

Cover art: Juan Mastromatteo
Cover design: Susan Pearce

LCCN: 2019930528
ISBN: 978-1-944585-31-0

Acknowledgments

A special thanks to the magazines in which the following poems appeared, sometimes in earlier versions with different titles:

ACM (*Another Chicago Magazine*): "Para seguir enrabando" / "Staying Connected," "Remontando" / "Kite-flying" and "Poema de amor" / "Love Poem"
Blue Lyra Review: "Tentáculos" / "Tentacles," and "A una vigilia del desmayo" / "Mourning by Fainting"
Chattahoochee Review: "En la cabeza"/ "In Your Head" and "Hemisferios" / "Hemispheres"
Crazyhorse: "Detrás del diseño" /"Behind the Design"
Diode: "El cuarto de Adriana" / "Adriana's Room," "Cantos," / "Corners," "Me toca a mí hoy," / "My Turn Today," "Estrategias" / "Strategies" and "Writing" / "Escribir"
Drunken Boat: "Versatilidad" / "Versatility," "Recorridos" / "Journeys" and "Reencarnación" / "Reincarnation"
eleven eleven: "De Rusia a Lituania una frutilla" / "From Russia to Lithuania: A Strawberry"
Fourteen Hills: "Insurgencia" / "Mutiny"
Gargoyle: "Studying in a Cafe" and "Without Words"
Hayden's Ferry: "Calendar," "Moving," and "Laundry Line"
International Poetry Review: "Le Coquelicot: La amapola de Van Dongen," / "Le Coquelicot: The Corn Poppy by Van Dongen" and "Antropología" / "Anthropology"
Michigan Quarterly Review: "Preguntas con frutillas" / "Questions with Strawberries," "Recobrando la cosmética" / "Makeover" and "Mojarme mientras caen las gotas" / "Getting Wet as Raindrops Fall"
Reunion: The Dallas Review: "Comings and Goings"
Southeast Review: "The Rain Initiates Directions" and "Question"
Taos Journal of Art and Poetry: "Corporizando el temblor" / "Embody the Tremor"
Texas Review: "Clues" and "Coming to Terms"
Visions International: "En concierto" / "In Concert" and "Brilla en la oscuridad" / "Glow in the Dark"

We are also grateful to the publishing house Yaugurú (Montevideo, Uruguay), which published *Los brazos del saguaro* (2015), on which this book is based.

Contents

Preface by Barbara Goldberg   9
Introduction by Jesse Lee Kercheval   11
About the Translation by Catherine Jagoe   14

FIN *TERMINA CON LA BOCA CERRADA* /
THE *END* ENDS WITH YOUR MOUTH CLOSED
    Sin palabras / Without Words   18
    Dolor / Grief   20
    Versatilidad / Versatility   22
    Calendario I / Calendar I   24
    Recorridos / Journeys   26
    Me toca a mí hoy / My Turn Today   28
    Distancias / Distances   30
    Reencarnación / Reincarnation   32

VOLVER EN TINTA / REBORN IN INK
    Estrategias / Strategies   36
    Estudiando en un café / Studying in a Cafe   38
    Escribir / Writing   40
    Insurgencia / Mutiny   42
    Indicios / Clues   44
    Cantos / Corners   46
    Remontando / Kite-flying   48
    El cuarto de Adriana / Adriana's Room   50
    Este lavado / Laundry Line   52
    Recobrando la cosmética / Makeover   54
    A una vigilia del desmayo / Mourning by Fainting   56
    Calendario II / Calendar II   58
    Para seguir enrabando / Staying Connected   60
    Mudanza / Moving   62

LO COTIDIANO DE UN PIERCING / THE SHARP EDGE OF EVERY DAY
    De Rusia a Lituania una frutilla /
       From Russia to Lithuania: A Strawberry   66
    Preguntas con frutillas / Questions with Strawberries   68

Pecosa / Freckled   70
Modus vivendi / Modus vivendi   72
Siempre ahí / Always There   74
Brilla en la oscuridad / Glow in the Dark   76
Antropología / Anthropology   78
Le Coquelicot: La amapola de Van Dongen / Le
       Coquelicot: The Corn Poppy by Van Dongen   80
Corporizando el temblor / Embody the Tremor   82
Agencia / Agency   84
Voz / Voice   86
En la cabeza / In Your Head   88
Poema de amor / Love Poem   90
La lluvia inicia direcciones / The Rain Initiates Directions   92
Pregunta / Question   94
Asumirse / Coming to Terms   96

Longitudes y latitudes / Longitudes and Latitudes
    Si la tormente puede / If Only the Storm   100
    Secretos / Secrets   102
    El mar empieza en la orilla /
       The Sea Begins at the Shore   104
    Idas y venidas / Comings and Goings   106
    Brújula / Compass   108
    Hemisferios / Hemispheres   110
    Mojarme mientras caen las gotas /
       Getting Wet As Raindrops Fall   112
    En concierto / In Concert   114
    Detrás del diseño / Behind the Design   116
    Sin romanticismo / No Romanticizing   118
    Tentáculos / Tentacles   120
    Salvo los huecos / Except for the Holes   122
    Los números / Numbers   124

About the Author, Translators, and Artist   127
About The Word Works   129
Other Word Works Books   130

Preface

Something strange is going on with the language in Laura Cesarco Eglin's poems. Not the words themselves—they are simple and direct. Rather, it is the zig-zag rhythms, the stop and go, the erratic punctuation. The poems stutter in their attempt to find their way.

Stuttering delays closure. And the death of Cesarco Eglin's father remains an open wound. The poems here describe the gravitational force of her grief, pulling language along with a sense of self into a black hole.

Grief fractures time, making continuity intermittent— hence the stop and go. Grief also fractures the poet's confidence. "There is no trail without you…" refers to Cesarco Eglin's father, who glued stars on her ceiling when she was a child, stars that "framed and spangled" her nights ("Glow in the Dark"). But now she feels lost, dislocated: "I cannot connect the dots."

Feeling disconnected is translated into text—sometimes periods indicate full stops, sometimes not; sometimes line-breaks seem arbitrary, sometimes not. "[T]here here in this dream I" and "in all these layers of snow everything" are lines found in Cesarco Eglin's "Writing." She's expressing frustration at her inability to find the words of a phrase racing through her head. The lines reflect how the poet interrupts herself, leaving the reader to put the poem together from context. I find them startling, even beautiful. And once you notice the sentence fragments you hear Cesarco Eglin's strange and singular music.

Most painful for a poet is to feel cut off from language, the inability to find refuge in words, or even being able to hear. There are "snowflakes" in her ear. In "Mourning by Fainting" she describes how "the throbbing / I feel in my eardrums was / in my heart not long ago." She might as well be buried in ice, incommunicado.

Slowly, and with great difficulty, something does manage to rise to the surface, a phrase that keeps repeating itself, but stays hidden "in all these layers of snow everything / white like a page with no words" until the phrase is reborn in ink.

This collection reflects the resurgence of Cesarco Eglin's art—sorrow may make us mute, but poems can get born again in ink.

Barbara Goldberg
Washington, DC

Introduction

I first read Laura Cesarco Eglin's poetry when I was searching for poets to include in *América invertida: An Anthology of Emerging Uruguayan Poets* (University of New Mexico Press, 2016). When I read her first book, *Llamar al agua por su nombre* (Mouthfeel Press, 2010), I fell in love with Cesarco Eglin's work and knew she belonged in the anthology. I was impressed by the history and emotion of her second book, *Sastrería* (Yaugurú, 2011), with its poems about her maternal grandparents who were Holocaust survivors. When her third book, *Los brazos del saguaro* (Yaugurú, 2015), was published in Uruguay, I decided she was a poet I wanted to translate at length. I asked Catherine Jagoe to join me in the project and the result is *Reborn in Ink*, a revised version of *Los brazos del saguaro*.

Uruguay, with only 3.5 million people, is the smallest Spanish-speaking country in South America. It looks small on the map, tucked between its two giant neighbors, Brazil and Argentina. But Uruguayans do not like to think of their country as small. "On the map, surrounded by its large neighbors, Uruguay seems tiny," wrote the Uruguayan journalist Eduardo Galeano. "But not really. We have five times more land than Holland and five times fewer inhabitants. We have more cultivable land than Japan, and a population forty times smaller." Independent since 1825, Uruguay is a country of immigrants who came in waves from Spain, Italy, France, Russia, England, with half settling in the capital Montevideo, rather than Galeano's cultivatable countryside, though the backbone of Uruguayan economy has always been cattle and agriculture. Laura Cesarco Eglin's grandparents came from Czechoslovakia, Lithuania, and neighboring Argentina to settle in Montevideo. The Uruguayan artist Juan Mastromatteo, whose painting "Raigambre" is on the cover, emigrated from Italy as a child in 1950. Their family stories are typical of Uruguay.

Since the beginning, Uruguay has been a country of poets, many with roots both South American and in Europe. Both Isadore Ducasse (1846-1870), who wrote under the pen name Comte de Lautréamont and became the inspiration for the French surrealists, and the symbolist Jules Laforgue (1860-1887) were born and spent their boyhoods in Uruguay but became better known as French poets. Throughout much of the 20th century Uruguay was one of Latin America's most progressive societies, notable for its political stability, universal education, separation of religion and state, and large middle class. These favorable conditions produced generations of women poets. Juana de Ibarbourou (1885-1979) and Delmira Agustini (1886-1914) were among the first. They were joined by a group that became important around the Second World War. This Generation of '45 included Amanda Berenguer (1921-2010), Idea Vilariño (1920-2009), and Ida Vitale (1923-), and this tradition of women poets runs unbroken down to the present. Laura Cesarco Eglin is a wonderful addition to that distinguished line.

Laura Cesarco Eglin was born in Montevideo in 1976. She grew up there but went to university in Israel. Then, knowing she wanted to be a writer, she went to the University of Texas at El Paso for its bilingual M.F.A. in Creative Writing where she wrote many of the poems in this book. Despite these relocations, she is very much an Uruguayan poet. Once I found her, she put me in touch with other young poets whose work I wanted in *América invertida*. We finally met face to face in 2014 when she was in Uruguay visiting her mother and twin sister and I was there on a research semester. She participated in a reading to celebrate the completion of the translations for *América invertida* at the Uruguayan National Library. Since then we have met regularly—sometimes in Montevideo, sometimes in the United States. In 2015, she founded her own small press, Veliz Books, with Minerva Laveaga Luna. Veliz publishes books written in English and also books translated from Spanish, Portuguese, or Galician, cultivating artistic and literary connections that transcend geographical, cultural, and political borders. Cesarco Eglin is a translator as well. Her English translation of the Brazilian poet Hilda Hilst's *Of Death. Minimal Odes* was published in 2018 by co•im•press.

    I stress the history of Uruguay as a nation of immigrants and Cesarco Eglin's travels, countries, and languages (Spanish, Portuguese, English, and Hebrew) because I think this history and her life makes a larger point. With work in translation, we can feel distant from the author, as though she were someone living long ago and far away, someone who is different from ourselves, living in a fairy tale, in a world where "magical realism" is reality. But people have always crossed borders. Cesarco Eglin's grandparents, Holocaust survivors who left the camps first for Italy, then Uruguay, are the embodiment of this. And Laura Cesarco Eglin is a poet very much alive and present, writing, translating, and participating in the poetic life in both Uruguay and the United States. Her poems speak about her past, her family's past, but also our common world, here and now.

    This is why we chose the painting "Raigambre" by Uruguayan artist Juan Mastromatteo for the cover. The painting is part of a series where themes of life and death are combined with landscape and nature. And *raigambre* means a network of roots in Spanish, in both the literal sense (the roots of the tree go very deep) and the more metaphorical sense (the roots of Uruguayan poetry reach back to the beginning of the country). In the painting, the roots are the ghostly figures—our ancestors? descendents?—who wait below the landscape of rolling Uruguayan hills. Cesarco Eglin's poetry grows from deep roots and reaches up through the dense grass and onto the page.

    Jesse Lee Kercheval
    Madison, Wisconsin

About the Translation

Diane Seuss wrote recently that "[i]t is what can't be known, what can't be translated, the unspeakable, that is most potent in poetry. This is its irony, its strangeness—that a thing made of words is often about what cannot be said." Laura Cesarco Eglin's enigmatic and haunting poetry of grief, deracination, and modernity highlights the elusiveness of language and meaning, creating what she calls "spaces / for mystery." Her work is extremely difficult to translate, although at first glance it appears deceptively simple. The poet deliberately removes many of the conventional signposts to the reader, using little punctuation and sometimes ending mid-sentence. She exploits the flexibility of Spanish syntax, which does not need to append a pronoun to every verb, since the person is already signaled by the verb ending. This allows her to run phrases together concertina-fashion, inviting simultaneous but different readings of certain passages. The challenge for English speakers is that we must have a pronoun before every verb: we have to specify who is performing it, and for third-person verbs we cannot leave the gender open, but must decide between "she," "he," and "it" or possibly "one" or "you." In poems such as "Compass," "The Rain Initiates Directions," and "Except for the Holes," several of the verbs are impersonal in Spanish, but have to be assigned a personal pronoun in the English.

These poems are also challenging to render in English because they contain cultural references that might not be obvious to an American audience. They evoke Uruguayan experience—as in the tango lyrics in "My Turn Today"—and also the Holocaust, for example in the poem "Makeover," which obliquely refers to the way that prisoners in Nazi concentration camps tried to make themselves look rosy-cheeked and healthy at roll-call in order not to be sent to the line of inmates destined for the gas chambers. In the original version of "Tentacles," she uses three different Spanish words for "jellyfish," two of which, *aguaviva* and *malagua*, contain references to water (literally, "living water" and "bad water"). This sets up a chain of images of being embraced by animate water that is impossible to replicate entirely in English.

Several poems exploit the sonics of Spanish: the prose poem "Reincarnation" riffs on the Spanish word for tomb, *tumba*, which ends in a vowel, "a," which means that the mouth is open at the end of the word. English words associated with death—tomb, corpse, grave, morgue—end with consonants and the mouth closed, so we had to rely on the image of the reader opening the mouth to take the next breath to convey the notion of openness. In that poem, too, the author is exploiting polysemy in her mother tongue: *tumba* (tomb) echoes *retumbar* (to reverberate), and *encantamiento* (enchantment, spell) is then echoed by *canto* (stone and also chant/song/poem).

The translation challenges in this book are epitomized in the one-line poem "Grief." In Spanish, the word *dolor* can mean both pain and grief. The poem's three short statements—all variations of the same verb—play on the multiple meanings of *doler* (to hurt) in Spanish. In English, while pain and grief are clearly related, they are not contained in one word, so the act of translation forces us to choose between them, and the secondary or related echoes of meaning within the original words are not matched by corresponding associations in English. The first sentence translates fairly simply as "It's not enough to say that something hurts [me]." But then the poet takes an impersonal, intransitive verb, and does something radical: she makes it personal and transitive. *Estoy doliendo* means literally "I am hurting"—but the unusualness of that linguistic choice, making an impersonal verb personal, is lost in English. The last sentence of the poem is simply one first-person verb, even more radically personal and active yet: *Duelo*. One can translate this as "I hurt," but again, we lose the iconoclasm, the fact that it is never used as an active verb, and the double meanings: *duelo* is also a noun, meaning two things: "mourning" and "duel." The poet has managed to make pain an active form of grief that the speaker embodies, in a way that stretches and challenges ordinary language. It is a meditation on the nature of the grieving process, powerfully encapsulated in a few relatively simple words. It is also a reflection on the way physical pain (which surfaces so often in this book) is also an experience of loss and mourning. The English version—whether we choose pain or grief as our primary meaning—falls flat in comparison.

As far as possible, we have sought to respect the mysterious, elliptical nature of the Spanish poems and to mirror the spare beauty of Cesarco Eglin's language and imagery.

Catherine Jagoe
Madison, Wisconsin

FIN *TERMINA CON LA BOCA CERRADA*

The *End* Ends with Your Mouth Closed

Sin palabras

Las cicatrices son ideogramas
que acompañan tu historia
ellas me abren anécdotas
para rastrearme en sus relieves
recorro con mis dedos
y me las aprendo de memoria

* * *

Si la sombra alcanza a desaparecer
mi boca, no es cuestión
de esperar que pasen las horas
y se reacomode el sol:
en ese mismo lugar en un ya
las sombras se rayan con mi voz

* * *

Alcanzo a entender la desesperanza
son dolores agudos que obligan
a juntar las pestañas
las lágrimas incrustadas en la garganta
para que no las vean llanto para que no
te vea pensando en decirme
que estás por cerrar los ojos

Without Words

The scars are pictographs
to go with your history
they offer me stories
let me trace myself in their raised outlines
I run my fingers over them
and learn them by heart

       * * *

If the shadow advances, erases
my mouth, it is not a question
of hoping the hours will pass
and the sun will move:
in that same place in the now
my voice splits the shadows.

       * * *

I've come to understand despair
it's a sharp ache that makes me
blink hard
tears wedged in my throat
so no one will see me crying so
I won't see you thinking about telling me
you're about to close your eyes

Dolor

No basta decir que algo me duele. Estoy doliendo. Duelo.

Grief

It is not enough to say it hurts. I'm aching. Stricken.

Versatilidad

　　　　　　　　　　　　　　Tu muerte se aparece de muchas formas. La suavidad de los pétalos guarda lo duro de un cuerpo. El mar te tiene en cada onda enseñándome todavía a navegar. Ese de repente que se define con lágrimas que buscan siempre un lugar distinto donde manifestarse. El 8 pesa más que los otros días del mes. Tu muerte es no tener a alguien conmigo que elija sambayón en una heladería. La voz del mate matinal lavándose en la memoria. Los sueños que recobran vida a la muerte le abren posibilidades, le exigen a la vigilia los personajes que desechó. Las postales y cartas que te mandé no tendrían que estar nuevamente en mis manos. Los sellos perdidos en un recorrido que los desconcierta.

Versatility

Your death appears in many forms. The softness of petals holds the hard fact of a body. The sea with you on every wave still teaching me to navigate. Sudden tears always searching for a different place to emerge. The 8th weighs more than the other days of the month. Your death is not having someone with me who chooses eggnog flavor in an ice cream parlor. Your voice like morning *mate* diluted by memory as the day wears on. Dreams that bring back the living from the dead, open up possibilities, demand the waking hours yield up the lost. The postcards and letters that I sent you should not have returned to my hands. Their stamps lost on a bewildering journey.

Calendario I

clama lo que parece
plano y negro. Dibujo
que apuesto a levantarlo
liviano y tanto peso me
desmonta mientras clama
en la ausencia de color y la presencia
insiste en que está ahí
para quedarse, clama. El dolor
tiene sonido el dolor crece en sentidos
lo que parece clama hasta aparecer
que lo mudo se calla cada mes en relación
a noviembre clama que el 8 vuelve
varias veces por año clama varias veces
a decírmelo con la firmeza de
siempre clama.

Calendar I

Its flat blackness
cries out. A chart
I try to lift, assuming it will be
light, and its weight
undoes me as it cries out
in the absence of color. Its presence
insists that it's here
to stay, crying out. Pain
has a sound, pain grows in ways
that seem to cry out until it appears
the muffled grows quieter every month.
In November it cries out that the 8th returns
many times a year, cries out over and over
insisting, adamant,
always crying out.

Recorridos

Voy abriendo tu nombre
despacio, intentando
volver a él de alguna manera
el entresueño me lo brindó
como la brisa, un aroma
que aletea yéndose aun
sin terminar de llegar y cuando despierto
abro los ojos
despacio para no perder el recuerdo
tuyo donde cada letra
tenía sentido y se apalabraban
a la red de venas—directo a la raíz
entendía la trayectoria
que hoy se resiste,
a veces, la palabra en desuso
muere, a veces cambia

Journeys

I keep unwrapping your name
slowly, attempting
to return to it somehow
drowsiness brought it to me
like a breeze, a scent
that wafts away leaving without
ever really arriving and when I wake
I open my eyes
slowly so as not to lose the memory
of you in which every letter
made sense and corresponded
to my network of veins—down to the root
I used to understand the trajectory
but today it's resistant,
a word in disuse
sometimes dies, sometimes changes

Me toca a mí hoy

Aquellos tiempos son estos pero
diferentes ahora y mañana otro tanto
cuando cante yo *Adiós*
muchachos, compañeros de mi vida,
barra querida de aquellos tiempos
y otro aprenda este tango
y se lo lleve consigo mientras me alejo
con el tiempo de emprender la retirada
de alejarme de la muchachada
prendo radio Clarín 580 AM
para resistir con el cuerpo y dejarme ir

My Turn Today

Those times are now these days
but different and tomorrow they'll be even more so
I'll be singing *So long,*
boys, companions of my life,
the gang from the old days
and someone else will learn this tango
and take it with them while I move on
in time to beat a retreat
and move away from you all
I turn the radio to Clarín 580 AM
my body resisting but also letting go

Distancias

Tu nombre a larga distancia está
tan cerca como saberlo decir.

Distances

Your name at a great distance is
almost close enough to say.

Reencarnación

Tumba es aguantar la respiración mientras dejamos que vibre e inmediatamente empujar la boca con desespero a abrirse porque no alcanza el aliento para tanta soledad. Un eco que engaña al vacío— la voz del silencio: retumba. La tierra también. De ahí y hacia ahí es un reflejo, como el encantamiento que lo causa. Desde la muerte se entiende el canto. Desde el canto se desecha la palabra fin. Alguien se equivocó con el significado porque si quisiera que fuera un fin terminaría con la boca cerrada.

Reincarnation

Tomb is pronounced by holding the breath and letting it vibrate, and immediately, desperately, forcing the mouth open because there is not enough breath for that much loneliness. An echo that fools the emptiness—the voice of silence: it reverberates. The earth too. From here to there is a reflex, like the spell that causes it. From the tomb, the poem is understood. In the poem, the end is undone. Someone got the meaning wrong. If this was meant to be the end, it would end with your mouth closed.

VOLVER EN TINTA

Reborn in Ink

Estrategias

Me prometí despertarme
a las 6:33 a.m. para tener tiempo
de volverme a dormir volverme
a despertar dormida y más
apurada pero habiéndole robado
a la mañana un espacio, habiéndole
dedicado un descanso al apuro. Pausar
entre piso y piso: cambiar de idioma es
andar en otra frecuencia y desahogar
las ganas de poner la diéresis. El lujo
de lo paralelo es apoyar el pie.

El nudo y el desenredo están
en el mismo hilo el ánimo
del cabello al florecer
sin pétalos es en realidad
marchitar no es más que exigirle
a un verbo que lo haga otro:
en ese momento estoy
ocupada para conjugarme en
oraciones, en ese momento
un momento.

Strategies

I vowed to wake
at 6:33 a.m. so I'd have time
to fall back asleep and wake
sleepy again, more rushed
but having stolen a space
from the morning, given
rushing a rest. A pause
between floors: switching languages means
proceeding on another frequency, indulging
the urge to insert a line-break. The luxury
of the parallel is firm footing.

The knot and the unraveling happen
to the same strand the spirit
of a hair splitting
open is really
withering, it's merely demanding
another verb act for it:
at this moment I'm
too busy to conjugate myself
in sentences, at this moment
one moment.

Estudiando en un café

Ese alféizar marrón es el comienzo. Quedarme
mirando un florero de vidrio que obliga a cortar
los dos tallos que sostienen su margarita. Una mirada
cada vez que termino una oración, como leer
entre líneas, como entender que las pausas hacen
a la lectura.

Studying in a Cafe

This brown windowsill is the beginning. I keep
gazing at a glass flower vase that insists on splitting
the stem of a daisy in two. Gazing
every time I finish a sentence, as if reading
between the lines, as if understanding the pauses make
the reading.

Escribir

Se repite una frase. Todavía
no sé cuál es
la oigo venir se instala
más allá de lo que digan
yo la trato de escuchar—hay algo
ahí acá en este sueño yo
la digo en secreto y el secreto
no me susurra a mí se guarda
en todas estas capas de nieve todo
blanco como una hoja sin letras ya
está empezada en la cabeza y la frase
se escribe con el contraste por eso
guardo silencio. Atenta
lo desparramo cuando es necesario:
copos de nieve, los oídos
a toda máquina la frase
vuelve en tinta

Writing

A phrase is repeating itself. I don't
yet know what it is
I can hear it coming, settling in
somewhere beyond the spoken word
I try to listen for it—there's something
there here in this dream I
can say it in secret but the secret
doesn't whisper back, it stays hidden
in all these layers of snow everything
white like a page with no words yet
it's starting in my head the phrase
will write itself in contrast that's why
I stay silent. If I pay attention
it will spill out when needed:
snowflakes, my ears
straining to hear it, the phrase
reborn in ink

Insurgencia

Me creció un pomelo
en el estómago, hace ya
unos días que decide
en qué dirección abrirá
los gajos, los tejidos que
van a rasgarse, los que se van
a acomodar. Y no tengo
que hacer nada de eso.
Un pomelo entiende y yo
no irrumpo. Esto es un capítulo
aparte de la digestión. Si observo bien
adentro, cada bolsita de jugo—
la poética de lo amargo tiene color
amarillo. Invita a hacerme de
filamentos, agasajar así
al pomelo, escucharlo.

Mutiny

A grapefruit has grown
in my stomach; it's been
deciding for some days
which way the segments will open
which tissues
will be torn, which
rearranged. I don't
have to do anything.
A grapefruit understands and I
won't interrupt. This is separate
from the chapter on digestion. If I look hard
inside, every bit of juice—
the poetics of bitterness is
yellow. It invites me to become
filaments, to welcome
the grapefruit, listen to it.

Indicios

Le dedica tiempo
a las puntas de su cabello
aceitándolas contra el florecimiento
esos quiebres son demasiado

Entre los dedos cabe acariciar
un pétalo bajo la insistencia
de incorporar suavidad

Hay que fijarse de qué forma
descifran el mensaje que leyeron
en los cuerpos. Eso también
es una marca

Un punto siempre lleva
a un desarrollo porque desde
el vamos que se fue
se acabó

Cuando afirmó la mordida tuvo
el gesto de dejarse morir
y no se sabe bien
cuántas lágrimas arman
un buen llanto

Clues

She spends time
on her split ends
oiling them to stop the splitting
the breakage is too much

It's possible to rub
a petal between your fingers
insist on embodying softness

Notice how the fingers
decipher the message they read
in bodies. That too
is a clue

An end point always develops
into something because
it's all been over
since the get-go

When he clenched his teeth he
was kind enough to let himself die
and no one knows for sure
how many tears there are
in a good cry

Cantos

Respirar en el minuto tres
es tener la pierna para patear
una piedrita en la calle hacia
la esquina de un arco
como lo improvisto sin plan está
el mundial en todo canto.

Abro los ojos hacia la ventana el sol
se pinta en la punta superior izquierda
la mañana también ofrece celeste con
volado blanco como la espuma de la clara
haciendo olas antes que la yema
difumine el degradé en la ventana.

Así sé que el día existe
como día y no
como tantas horas.

El punto de fuga de la bañera
es el tapón en mi mano. El agua
se va en remolinos el hemisferio
elige la dirección. Otros remolinos
dan la crecida al pelo—nací con dos
sabiendo la necesidad de
un respaldo en caso de quimio atar
los mechones de lana en un nudo
paralelo a la garganta, paralelos no
se juntan en la pelada.

Esta repetición es la mañana
que necesitaba pensar para no volver
toda esquina parte del ring.

En las esquinas tiende a juntarse
lo que después barro.

Corners

Taking a breath after three minutes
is like having a leg to kick
a pebble in the street towards
the corner of a goal
like the unforeseen unplanned
the world cup is in every pebble.

I open my eyes to look at the window the sun
is painted in the top left-hand corner
the morning offers sky-blue with
ruffles of foamy egg-white
rippling before the sun's yolk-yellow
makes the color gradient in the window fade away.

That's how I know the day
exists as a day and not
as so many hours.

The escape hatch in the bath
is the plug in my hand. The water
swirls down the hemisphere
dictates the direction. Hair grows
in swirls too—I was born with double
crowns knowing the need
for backup in case of chemo I could tie
hanks of wool in a knot
parallel to the lump in my throat, parallels
that won't meet on my bald head.

This repetition is the morning
I needed in order to think, so as not to turn
every corner into a boxing ring.

What gathers in the corners
I will sweep up later.

Remontando

Este dolor de cabeza se instaló
subrepticiamente y lo sé porque sigo
preguntándome cómo puede ser un dolor
de cabeza en la mañana
todo va más lento y con más
cuidado me hace observar
las cejas se hacen más tangibles
albergando curvatura fruncida que

aliso y conecto con inmensidad
un plano con rastros; el codo
un vértice también participa
lleva mi mano a la frente
y a los ojos a cerrarse si la mano
pesa entonces no cumple, impone
quiero que toque más allá de rozar más
lejos que un pesar la conglomeración
se despeja a escondidas; seguir deteniéndome
ante el apuro, coordino la tensión
perfecta del hilo entre la mano y la cometa.

Kite-flying

This headache set in
surreptitiously I know because I keep
wondering how you can get
a headache in the morning
everything goes more slowly and
carefully it makes me notice
my eyebrows become more tangible
harboring the curve of a frown that

I smooth out, connecting with immensity
a smooth surface with tracks; my elbow
is part of it too, an apex
that raises my hand to my forehead
and closes my eyes. If the hand
is heavy it won't work, too overbearing
I crave a little more than a caress
but not enough to regret, the dense cluster
clears, unseen; I need to keep pausing
whenever I'm rushed, keeping
the kite-string in my hand perfectly taut.

El cuarto de Adriana

Las geografías de su cuarto
me aseguraban que debajo
de las montañas del otro lado
del vidrio del auto no había más
que su ropa sucia. En realidad
el paisaje dictaminaba pradera
pero aquel cuarto reorganizaba
el concepto de imaginación. El punto
de partida a las arrugas de un elefante,
en un primer plano, por supuesto
la orilla de la alfombra difiere de la costa
y desintegra un límite arando
el espacio por el que se cuela otro
momento, entre aspas cabe el molino
y las comillas. La expresión de
amor propio de tocarse el cuello
al peinarse. En ese cuarto
aprendí la idiosincrasia en comunidad.

Adriana's Room

for my twin sister

The geographies of her room
assured me there was nothing
under the mountains on the other side
of the car window except
her dirty clothes. In fact
the landscape evoked the prairie
but that room reorganized
my idea of imagination. The shore
of the rug in the foreground,
the starting point, wrinkled as an elephant,
is not the coast, of course
and it erases the boundary, plowing
a space through which another
moment squeezes, between quotation marks,
raised eyebrows. Self-care
means touching your own neck
while brushing your hair. In that room
I learned eccentricity in community.

Este lavado

Las sombras son otras historias
de cuajo el hombre con las manos
en los bolsillos de un traje curvándole
los hombros y la mujer a la que le veo
su embarazo sé que está moviendo
las manos al hablar y por último
el tótem indígena trabajado
en madera, trabajando, hasta que descuelgo
las tres camisas que dejé secando; algo debo
vestirme y por qué no embarazarme
desde la cuerda a mi postura en la línea
que describe el arqueo de
la espalda protuberando la gestación
la forma en que muevo las manos
para trabajar la línea diciéndome
que hoy soy ésta y corporizo
la emoción de quienes aparecerán.

Laundry Line

The shadows are other stories
altogether: the man with his hands
in the pockets of his suit, making him
hunch his shoulders, and the woman
whose pregnancy I notice is waving
her hands as she speaks and then there's
the Indian totem carved in wood
until I take down the three shirts
I hung to dry; I must
put some clothes on and why not get pregnant
from the laundry line to my posture in line
my back describes an arch
that makes my belly bulge as if gestating
the way I move my hands
to work the line telling myself
today I'll be this one and embody
the feelings of people yet to come.

Recobrando la cosmética

Lápiz de labio azul para conmemorar
los días de frío severo de uñas
moradas y labios haciendo juego
cuando está cansada y se pinta
sombras donde las ojeras
deberían estar, se sabe libre
de marcar la ascendente del ánimo
el lápiz de labio rojo en la cartera
es la herramienta de emergencia
por si un día su palidez la coloca
en el lado equivocado
unos toques en el cachete cambian
el pronóstico de vida es otro
el rosado como álter ego
en el borde del vaso cuando no está
pronta para dejar
el lugar del que se fue
los días con rímel le dan más
contundencia al llanto, en esta pantalla
blanco y negro ideal para nostalgiar

Makeover

Blue lipstick in remembrance
of days of intense cold of nails
turning blue and lips to match
when she's tired she applies
eyeshadow where the bags under
her eyes should be, she feels free
to mark her spirits rising
the red lipstick in her purse
is a tool for emergencies
in case one day her pallor lands her
in the wrong line,
a few dabs on the cheeks can
alter your chance of survival
pink as an alter ego
on the rim of the glass when she's not
ready to let go
of the place she left
mascara days make her tears
more weighty, on this black
and white screen so perfect
for nostalgia

A una vigilia del desmayo

A veces despierto
y ya estoy mareada; cierro
los ojos nuevamente
y rebobino la película a pie
entendiendo que no hay nada
que la sangre no sepa; que no
hay nada que no titile
hasta lo continuo es
intermitente; una sacudida vacila la certeza
del piso al techo está la pared
rajada en una ola de peldaños entretenidos
agitando los escalones a subir despacio—rápido
a bajar al costado; aterrizaje forzoso
la gravedad distribuida en todas las direcciones
van las manos para atajar; el bombeo
que siento en el tímpano estaba
en el corazón hasta hace poco

Mourning by Fainting

At times I wake up
and I'm already dizzy; I close
my eyes again
rewinding the film step by step
knowing there's nothing
the blood doesn't know; nothing
that doesn't waver
even continuity is
intermittent; certainty can be jolted
the wall is cracked
from floor to ceiling in a wave of zig-zags
the stairs sway, ascend slowly—quick
go down sideways; forced landing
gravity distributed in all directions
my hands try to break my fall; the throbbing
I feel in my eardrums was
in my heart not long ago

Calendario II

Mientras todavía sea julio estoy
a salvo de salir corriendo y seguir
hasta no tenerle más miedo a estos
meses que antes pintaban acuarelas
que antes hablaban en azulejos mojados
después que los pinté abrí la boca
y entre cada pincelada un molar
prensil.

Calendar II

As long as it's still July I am
safe no need to run away keep going
till I no longer fear these
months that used to depict watercolors
that used to speak in wet tiles
after I painted them I opened my mouth
a prehensile molar between each brush
stroke.

Para seguir enrabando

el celular suena desde el fondo
de la cartera se hurga para llegar
a él. Se recorren las decisiones de
la mañana comparando con la caída
del sol y el comienzo de la brisa. Un contorno
salta en una definición y con eso
una historia. Lo cilíndrico del chapstick
alivia mientras en la mano, el cierre
de la billetera hace cosquillas al deseo
de desparramar más ansias de saber
que ahí no hay nada. Todo
está en tocar el traspaso de isla en isla
agregándole una *es* a *verdad* para que sean
tranquilamente muchas. Recobrando vidas
con la mano. Un mapa sin destino
marcado; dibujarle unas líneas entre
hallazgos surge el desequilibrio. Líneas
asomadas. El celular en mi mano
lo suelto

Staying Connected

the cellphone rings at the bottom
of your purse and you scramble to
reach it. You retrace the morning's
decisions comparing them with the
setting sun and rising breeze. An outline
suddenly becomes a definition and thus
a story. The tube of chapstick
is a relief in your hand, the snap
on your wallet piques your desire
to dispel more anxieties to know
there's nothing there. It's all
about touching, island-hopping
adding an "s" to "truth" so it can
multiply peacefully. Retrieving lives
with my hand. A map with no
destination marked; drawing lines between
discoveries leads to imbalance. Lines
peer out. I let the cellphone in my hand
go

Mundanza

Una caja cada día y los días de más ansiedad armo una más. Con cuidado coloco los libros para que no tropiecen las palabras, para que cuando abra las cajas reconozca las historias con sorpresa. En otras cajas amontono preocupaciones. Laten. Creo que no hay cinta scotch que las mantenga cerradas el tiempo suficiente, porque aunque ese día sea ágil y alcance a deshacerme de las palpitaciones antes de que destapen cosas peores, logran filtrarse como humo que impregna esta casa y todo lo que ahí hay. De la manera más sutil, mudan. Es mejor tal vez sentarme y juntarme a las cajas como el espejo se acerca a la cara del miope. Mirar bien, detenidamente. Respirar hasta exhalar. Soltar, como estos tatuajes que el sueño deja en mi brazo. Unos diseños raros que quiero interpretar antes que pasen desapercibidos. Veo la cabeza de un beagle. Snoopy mirando dos carpas. A una el viento le exige movimiento.

Moving

A box a day and on anxious days I pack one more. I put the books in carefully so the words won't stumble, so that when I open the boxes I'll be surprised to recognize the stories. I store my worries in other boxes. They lie there, beating. There's no Scotch tape that will keep them shut long enough, because even if I'm quick that day and manage to get over my palpitations before they unmask worse things, they manage to seep through like the smoke that impregnates this house and everything in it. In the subtlest way, they shift. Maybe it's best to sit down next to the boxes like a near-sighted person holding a mirror close to her face. Take a good, long look. Breathe in, breathe out. To let go, like the tattoos that sleep leaves on my arm. Peculiar patterns that I want to interpret before they disappear unnoticed. I see a beagle's head. Snoopy looking at two tents. The wind forces one to move.

LO COTIDIANO DE UN PIERCING
The Sharp Edge of Every Day

De Rusia a Lituania una frutilla

La única Rusia que conozco
está en *klubnika*—una frutilla
no es lo mismo cuando rasgo
la primera capa de piel roja
sabiendo que Rusia se fue en
las semillitas que la lengua a veces
toca, algunas
palabras, pero de algunas no se tiene
a Rusia, aunque hay algo en cómo
mi abuelo sostiene una frutilla
para dármela, cierra los ojos, los dos
pero sé que todo el tiempo está
pensando en mí que nunca
fui a Rusia, ni a Lituania, y como
frutillas como si todavía estuviera ahí

From Russia to Lithuania: A Strawberry

The only Russia I know
is *klubnika*—a strawberry
isn't the same when I pierce
the outer layer of red skin
knowing that Russia lies in
the little seeds the tongue sometimes
touches, the odd
word, but the odd word isn't
Russia, although there's something
in the way my grandpa hands me
a strawberry and closes both eyes
I know all along he's thinking
about me, how I've never
been to Russia or Lithuania, how
I eat strawberries as if I were still there

Preguntas con frutillas

¿Y si de una frutilla me olvido de su color rojo, de su forma, de su sabor y me concentro en la semillita que me queda entre los dientes? ¿Sabré la palabra? ¿Inventaré otra? ¿El recorrido de la lengua será semilla? ¿Volveré a la frutilla siendo yo? ¿Mis pecas cobrarán otro sentido cuando me queme el sol hasta el rojo?

Questions with Strawberries

What if I forget the strawberry's redness, its shape, its flavor, and concentrate on the little seed stuck between my teeth? Will I know the word? Invent another? Will the tongue's journey become a seed? When I go back to being a strawberry will I still be myself? Will my freckles take on another meaning when the sun burns me red?

Pecosa

En esa pestaña argumenté todos mis deseos
antes de besarla y pegarla a mi pecho
supe guardarla entre la camisa y la piel
para que se asimile al resto de las pecas
huellas de los dos dedos allegándole fantasías
y hoy que alguien quiere decirme que
mis ansias son manchas que debo sacarme
no anima más el pecho a la respiración
inscrita en marrón sobre blanco.

Freckled

On that eyelash I pinned all my hopes
before kissing it and gluing it to my chest
I learned to keep it between my shirt and my skin
so it could blend in with the rest of my freckles
tips of my fingers gathering fantasies
and now that someone keeps telling me
my anxieties are spots I must remove
my chest has lost its faith in breathing
inscribed in brown on white on my skin.

Modus vivendi

Talón punta talón
dijo la fisioterapeuta
que no me olvidara del quiebre
entre el tobillo y el empeine
debe haber una bailarina
entre talón punta talón
como si fuera fácil recordar
cómo caminar
y el movimiento de cadera
viene con talón punta talón
me asegura la femineidad
en cada paso que la punta quiera
volver. Imantar y repeler
son una sola realidad
talón punta talón dirige
la batuta en direccionalidad
se ausenta de una llegada, prefiriendo
la referencia ambulante
de un arco recortado
talón punta talón la flecha.

Modus vivendi

Heel toe heel
said the physical therapist
reminding me not to forget to flex
ankle to instep
there should be a ballerina
between heel toe heel
as if it were easy to remember
how to walk
and the hip movement
that comes with heel toe heel
guarantees my femininity
with each step the toes want
to start over. Attraction and repulsion
are a single reality
heel toe heel directs
the conductor's baton in a direction
that has no arrival, preferring
the ambulatory reference
of a high arch
heel toe heel the arrow.

Siempre ahí

Conozco los detalles del dolor
y a la vez, me los olvido
cuando no están. Al principio
voy lento. El miedo tiene ese don—
nos apura o nos enlentece. Un paso
en falso y el dolor no espera
ni al adverbio rápidamente; lastima
hasta el grito. Otra sorpresa—es el dolor
articulado. Aúllo. ¿Para ahuyentar?
Ni a la fisioterapeuta le puedo traducir
cómo los nervios me los despluman
tanto que palidecen todo. Lo demás
el dolor en todos sus detalles, en todos
los detalles. Lo agudo está. También
esas lágrimas que se escapan a la traducción
que son en realidad cómo lo digo—Ayudame.

Always There

I know the particulars of the pain
and yet I forget them
when they're not there. At first
I go slowly. Fear has a knack
of speeding us up or slowing us down. One false
step and the pain won't wait
even for the adverb quickly; it hurts
so much I cry out. Another surprise—the pain is
expressed. I howl. To drive it away?
I cannot even translate to the physical therapist
how my nerves are plucked
so hard that all else pales. The rest
the pain in all its particulars, in all
the particulars. The sharpness. Also
these tears that escape translation
but are in fact translated as I say—Help me.

Brilla en la oscuridad

Armaste una constelación para contrarrestar
la oscuridad de la noche y los días
deshojados; mis ojos que la aprecian
durante las horas con lentes e imaginan
la luminosidad del cielo sin

contrastes de luz y no
el gris está en la miopía; su capacidad
de desvanecer colores y formas —magia
como la que le pido a la primera
estrella que llego a ver
me conecta a mi deseo justamente
con los ojos cerrados

Vos que pegaste estrellitas y tu ida
dejó este techo para mí que hoy
arma mis noches, las constela
porque sin estela no estás vos, no
puedo unir los puntos

Glow in the Dark

You put up a constellation to counteract
the darkness at night and the leafless
days; my eyes appreciate it
when I'm wearing glasses and can imagine
the luminous sky without

contrasts of light and without
the gray that is myopia; its ability
to dim colors and forms—magic
like the kind I wish for on the first
star I see
it connects me to my wish only
when my eyes are closed

You glued those little stars up there
and although you're gone
you left me this ceiling that frames
my nights now, spangles them,
but because there is no trail without you, I
cannot connect the dots.

Antropología

Antes no sabía hablarle
a mi cuerpo. Creí conocerlo
porque me memoricé dos lunares
en la piel—la marca de mi
sexualidad.

La desconexión que sufre
por irremediable te obliga a armar
la llegada cada vez en otro lugar.
Aprendí que son dos cosas aparte:
el cuerpo y el tiempo.

Ya no miro por el agujero y espero
ver después lo que entendí en
una pantalla. Entre lo angosto
de uno y lo ancho del otro lo que
no se capta.

Te escucho. Ahora sí, un idioma
que sabía y no practicaba. Te hablo
sin la ansiedad que marcaba
el amanecer.

Anthropology

I didn't know how to talk
to my body before. I thought I knew it
because I'd memorized two moles
on my skin—marks of my
sexuality.

The irreparable disconnect the body suffers
forces you to deal with
arriving in a different place each time.
I learned they're two separate things:
the body and time.

I no longer peer through the hole hoping
to see what I learned
on a screen later. Between the narrowness
of the one and the immensity of the other
lies the imperceptible.

I hear you. Now at last, a language
I used to know but didn't practice. I speak to you
without the fear that used to mark
the dawn.

Le Coquelicot: La amapola de Van Dongen

Debo almacenar respiros
para imaginar a la mujer
en el cuadro, moviéndose
siendo ella. Voy a estudiar holandés
así poder darle
las palabras que precisa
me imantan a mirarla, mientras
ella, seria, observa sin parar
la combinación perfecta
entre el lápiz de labio y su gorro
lloro ante ella subvencionándole
lágrimas que guarda para un después
cuando quiera correr
el delineador, organizarse de otra manera
yo sigo coqueteando con la idea
traducir los ojos negros y reconciliar.

Le Coquelicot: The Corn Poppy by Van Dongen

I must hold my breath
to imagine the woman
in the painting glancing back,
being herself. I'm going to study Dutch
to give her the words she needs
to compel me to gaze at her, while
she, pensive, perpetually observes
the perfect match
between her lipstick and hat
I weep before her providing
tears that she saves for some later
time when her eyeliner might start
to run, to organize itself some other way
I continue flirting with the idea
translating and reconciling
those black eyes.

Corporizando el temblor

Cuando me concentro en una
parte, el estremecimiento

viene a recordar
que el cuerpo se siente
          qué más visual que el tacto
          de lo que casi se toca

¿Qué ritmo monto
para que lo subliminal cruce?
          un umbral se desata
          juntando partes, silbando movimiento

Embody the Tremor

When I focus on one
part, the shiver

comes as a reminder
that the body is felt
        what's more visual than the touch
        of what almost touches

What drumbeat shall I summon
so the subliminal can cross?
        a threshold is unmade
        by joining parts, whistling movement

Agencia

No necesito un caleidoscopio cuando puedo
acostarme con los ojos cerrados, la mirada dirigida
a una ventana y la respiración arma los vaivenes
de la luz, arma lo que no nombro para no darle
quietud, que siga pasando como a pesar de mí
aunque sé bien que cuando la montaña se derrita
y el corcho se ramifique estaré en Portugal; el viento
tironea para su lado, se desatan hojas, alguna que
otra bajo esta lapicera también indica cómo va
la corriente hoy sin necesidad de mojar la punta
del dedo para sentir de dónde viene
lo demás, no lo veo venir; está acá, ventrílocuo
del tiempo dice que yo digo que dice que digo
digo

Agency

I don't need a kaleidoscope when I can
lie down with my eyes closed, gazing out
the window while my breathing makes the light
come and go, creates what I do not name so as not
to exorcise it, may it go on happening in spite of me
though I know well enough that when the mountain melts
and the cork-trees leaf out I'll be in Portugal; the wind
blowing sideways, unleashing leaves, there are
a few under this pen to show which way the wind
blows today no need to wet my fingertip
to feel where it's coming from
as for the rest, I don't see what's coming; it's here, time's
ventriloquist says that I say that it says that I say
I say

Voz

Le sacó el badajo
a la campana para oírla
decirle cosas sólo a él

cerró su palma
la abrió
un pedazo de metal

Voice

He took the clapper
from the bell to hear it
say things to him alone

closed his palm
opened it
a piece of metal

En la cabeza

empiezo donde estoy
mirando tu espalda mientras lavás
los platos, escuchándote
que el apartamento está cableado
micrófonos escondidos
hay cosas que pasan acá.

Aguantar dos días más y el cuchillo
corta un poco, la esponja
el jabón tapa el procedimiento
se resbaló de tu mano
ese es el reporte que me cortó
el hombro en un gajo
hay cosas que pasan acá.

No sabía que me pasaban a mí
en la cabeza el cuchillo en tu mano.

In Your Head

I start where I am
looking at your back as you wash
the dishes, listening to you say
the apartment is wired
with hidden microphones
there are things happening here.

Hang on for two more days and the knife
cuts me a little, the sponge
and the soap suds hid what happened
it slipped out of your hand
that's the report that sliced
my shoulder open
there are things happening here.

I didn't know they were happening to me
in my head the knife in your hand.

Poema de amor

Qué lástima que no sabías.
¿Acaso no se escuchó por ahí?
Lo nuestro se acabó
con el fin de ver
hasta cuándo me iba
la pasión en rebrotes de amistad
y lo cotidiano de un piercing
al aseverar. Yo misma me clavo
la aguja para ver si duele.

No. No dolés. Yo te duelo a vos
en este duelo que empezás ahora
enterate que no siento amor.
Ése es mi duelo que me lastima
contigo un abrojo
arrancándole el olor al pasto
recién cortado, un pinchazo de anestesia
te desprendo y te tiro
lejos, hacia lo real.

Love Poem

What a shame you didn't know.
Perhaps you never got the news?
I'm breaking up with you
in order to see
how long passion lasts
we keep lapsing into friendship
and the sharp edge of every day
asserts itself. I prick myself with
the needle to see if it hurts.

No. You don't hurt. I hurt you
in this bereavement that you're beginning now
just know I don't feel love.
This is my mourning that wounds me
with you a brier
erasing the scent of fresh-cut grass
a prick of anesthesia
I pluck you out and throw you
a long way off, towards real life.

La lluvia inicia direcciones

Si me doy cuenta cuál es la primera gota
sabré cómo empieza la lluvia, qué cara tiene
como la luna cambia, la lluvia en ciclos
me moja de distinta forma, acude
con cinturas varias palabras todas
son algunas son de la lluvia encontrando
lonjas tocando como sólo la lluvia
puede caer de a poco caer a cántaros
la lluvia puede también irse y yo

The Rain Initiates Directions

If I can be aware of the very first drop
I'll know how the rain starts, how it looks
since the moon has phases, the rain in its cycles
drenches me in different ways, it comes
in various sizes all words
are few are the rain finding
its drumbeat playing as only the rain can
fall falling softly falling hard
the rain can disappear and so can I

Pregunta

I

No recuerdo quién
      era el día
que me preguntaron
quién soy

II

cuando tu piel
se junta con tu olor y tu voz
¿quién sos?

en estos fragmentos no sos más que yo
pensando en vos

Question

I

I don't remember who
      I was the day
they asked me
who I am

II

when your skin
joins your scent and your voice
who are you?

in these fragments you're no more than me
thinking of you

Asumirse

En la tarde, tarde, es tarde
para que el sol me lea el libro
y entienda el hilado fino del día

En la tarde, tarde, es tarde
para despedidas rotundas: el beso
borra lo que la mejilla en realidad absorbe

En la tarde, tarde, es tarde
ya no hay horas que me convenzan
que el respiro dura más
que el aleteo de una hoja de otoño

En la tarde, tarde, es tarde
y la noche carga
como la nube antes de desprenderse de la lluvia

En la tarde, tarde, es tarde
la decisión está tomada: atardecer
desde los primeros rayos de sol

En la tarde, tarde, es tarde
así, enhebrando el ojo que tiene que hacerlo
la tarde es tarde y yo soy yo

Coming to Terms

Late afternoon, late, it's late
for the sun to read me the book
for me to grasp the day's thin thread

Late afternoon, late, it's late
for last farewells: the kiss
erases what the cheek actually absorbs

Late afternoon, late, it's late
there's no time left to convince me
that breath lasts longer
than the flutter of a leaf in fall

Late afternoon, late, it's late
and the night is charged
like a cloud before it releases rain

Late afternoon, late, it's late
the decision's made: it's been getting dark
since the sun came up

Late afternoon, late, it's late
and so the needle must be threaded
the afternoon is late and I am me

LONGITUDES Y LATITUDES
Longitudes and Latitudes

Si la tormenta puede

Renata miraba porque no se le ocurría ningún otro verbo para aplicar a la situación. En algún momento el amarillo dejaría de ser sólo yema, y ella estaría ahí para percusionar el cambio. El tono de su nombre en cada persona comenzaba un tren y lo dirigía —algunos hacia el Este, llevándose el gris como quien cambia de hoja. No sabía cómo quedaba la estación después; eso de estar estática nunca la convenció y decidía cada vez no mirar atrás.

If Only the Storm

Renata was staring because she couldn't think of any other verb for the situation. At a certain point yellow would stop being only an egg-yolk, and she would be there rattling as it changed. The sound of her name spoken aloud always set a train in motion, driving it—some headed east, taking grayness with them as if turning a page. She didn't know what the station looked like afterwards; being stationary had never appealed to her and each time she decided not to look back.

Secretos

Después vinieron las nubes. El antes, como el sol, ya no se ve. Tampoco se ven las nubes. Ahora sólo un color: gris. No miro el cielo para confirmar la lluvia. Busco las gotas en la calle. El asfalto me lo va a decir todo. Lo sé. Él nunca se aguanta los secretos y menos uno como este. Las gotas son delatadas antes de sentirlas en la cabeza y hombros. En esas gotas, en todas, entiendo lo que guardaba. Muchos

Secrets

The clouds came afterwards. What was there before, like the sun, is now nowhere to be seen. Neither are the clouds. Now there's only one color: gray. I don't look at the sky to check if it's raining. I look for raindrops on the street. The asphalt will tell me everything, I know. It can never keep a secret, especially not one like this. It shows me raindrops before I feel them on my head and shoulders. In those droplets, in all of them, I understand what I was guarding. So much

El mar empieza en la orilla

Hizo traer bolsas llenas de bolitas de espuma plast. (¿Cómo es que en otros lugares no usan esta hermosa expresión? Nunca lo entendió.) Las rasgó para que nevara en el cuarto aunque no por eso las había comprado. Nevaba rápido, con todo el apuro de la gravedad, hasta que los copos de nieve fueron otra vez bolitas y cubrían todo el piso y a ella, de la punta del pie a la mitad del muslo. También practicaba hundir las manos—más allá de las muñecas, espuma, plast. Más que hundirse, aprendió a flotar, y después se animó a dar brazadas, y así, nadó. Nadó de una punta del cuarto a otra, en diagonal, en vertical, en horizontal, en redondo. Hizo hasta olas cuando se zambullía. Aguantaba la respiración cuando metía la cabeza entre la espuma plast, no vaya a ser que sin querer tragara alguna que otra bolita. Sostener el aliento, guardarlo para después. Guardarse a ella entre la espuma para respirar mejor. Atreverse a seguir aprendiendo las técnicas del agua, desde brazadas, clavados, a enriquecer el mar de espuma con una banda sonora del agua que alimentaban los días de verano en la playa. Una vez conquistada la espuma, los volados del mar, pensaría en la parte azul.

The Sea Begins at the Shore

She had bags of Styrofoam beads delivered. (Why is the lovely Uruguayan name for them, *espuma plast*, not used anywhere else? She's never understood.) She tore them open so it would snow in the room, although that's not why she bought them. It was snowing fast, with the urgency of gravity, until the snowflakes turned back into bits of Styrofoam covering the floor and her body, from the tips of her toes to the middle of her thighs. She practiced plunging her hands in them—up to the wrists, splashing in the foam. Instead of sinking, she learned to float, and then she got inspired to start paddling, and thus began to swim. She swam from one end of the room to the other, diagonally, vertically, horizontally, and in a circle. She even made waves when she dived in. She held her breath while submerging her head in the white foam, so as not to swallow some of the Styrofoam by accident. Holding her breath, saving it for later. She was submerging herself in the foam so as to breathe deeper. Daring to learn aquatic skills, strokes, dives, enriching the foamy sea with a sound track of water fed by summer days at the beach. Once she'd conquered the foam, the sea's ruffles, she'd think about the blue.

Idas y venidas

La L falla en mi teclado bajo mi fuerza. Dirección exacta: dedo anular, mano derecha, que no puede cumplir con hospedar ciertas palabras, que no puede decir. Se van a otros lados —ahí me llevan. Porque si de mi nombre queda sólo el aura, las cosas están cambiando. La L me habla de formular ajeno a mí, y así, insiste en mandarme en una ausencia plena. Salir de la lucha de resistencias. Salir. Entregarme al ni siquiera. Salirme. No se vuelve si el lugar es el mismo. No se es sin andar en verbo—cómo verbalizar

Comings and Goings

The L on my keyboard doesn't respond when I press it. Exact location: fourth finger, right hand. It cannot host certain words, cannot say them. They go elsewhere—taking me with them. Because if all that's left of my name is an aura, things are changing. The L speaks in formulas that are foreign to me, insists on sending me into a total absence. Oh to give up struggling to resist. To leave. To surrender to the Not Even. To get out. There's no return if the place is the same. There's no way to be without moving in a verb—how to verbalize

Brújula

Volver a dónde es
volver si no se entiende
que se ha ido. Dónde
como lugar inefable almacena
un equivalente en otros
de espaldas a él no hay
nada en el frente. Se va
se va a dónde si la vuelta
marca un antemano que al hablar
satisface la mano que toca
una nube. Así se explica dónde
va lo dicho, se junta
en silencio y después

Compass

How to return
if it's not understood
that you've left. The where
as an ineffable location holds
an equivalent in others
when you turn your back on it there is
nothing ahead. You go
you go where if the return
marks a before that when spoken
satisfies the hand that touches
a cloud. This explains
where words go when spoken
they gather in silence and then

Hemisferios

-10 °C de desierto me encuentran
en una latitud 34° 58' Sur donde
el verano lo calculan los dedos
en tres meses desde el 21 de diciembre
y me saco los guantes
porque el mar de febrero enseña
a bailar y en la arena reconocés tu agua
que la nieve concentra en blanco
donde los meses del verano son
dirección del invierno
enfría para hacer silencio y yo
también me hago en silencios

el frío amaina longitudes y latitudes

Hemispheres

15° F in the desert finds me
at a latitude of 34° 58' South where
summer can be counted on the fingers
it's three months starting December 21st
and I take off my gloves
because February's sea teaches
me how to dance and in the sand
you recognize your water
which the snow condenses into white
up north where the months of summer are
the address of winter
coldness breeds silence and I
too am made of silences

the cold shrinks longitudes and latitudes

Mojarme mientras caen las gotas

Le estoy perdiendo el miedo a la lluvia. Al fin empiezo a entender que el quid del asunto es el intermedio: estar mojada es una cosa, estar seca es otra, pero lo que nubla es estarse mojando, mojarse. La lluvia está separada del llover, y ahí en mi brazo, ahí donde el paraguas falla, se junta todo. Participar del cambio mientras hay un relato de cada paso que está afuera y lo incorporo. Cuando escampe voy a necesitar que empiece a llover nuevamente.

Getting Wet As Raindrops Fall

I'm losing my fear of the rain. At last I'm starting to understand that the issue is the halfway-point: being wet is one thing, being dry another, but what is nebulous is the getting wet itself. The rain is separate from raining, and there on my arm, beyond the umbrella's reach, it all comes together. To participate in change while there's a narrative of each step out there that I embody. When it clears up I'm going to need it to start raining all over again.

En concierto

La diferencia entre una viola y un violín
no existe para alguien
no entrenado, y menos
desde la fila 33, el cartelito de la butaca
17 tampoco se distinguía bien y ese sí
fue importante ver. Determinó
el punto de vista. Cerré los ojos
y escuché las palabras venir.

In Concert

The difference between a viola and a violin
doesn't exist for one
untrained, still less
in row 33, the little number-plate
on seat 17 was difficult to see too and
it was important to see that. It determined
the point of view. I closed my eyes
and listened to the words arrive.

Detrás del diseño

Hay quienes pegarían
la bibliotequita a la pared
para aprovechar el espacio
agregarle a la mayoría, cerrar
el corredor cerrar la válvula
es la magia de desaparecer un algo
que es lo que vale la pena del
sombrero del mago—algo

Cuánto debe circular
entre la pared y la bibliotequita
son espacios
para el misterio. Se acumula
sin idea de cantidad. Es dejar
también un refugio al escape
el concepto de posibilidad sabe
evitar la claustrofobia

Behind the Design

Some people would put
the bookshelf next to the wall
to make more space
to maximize it, closing
the corridor like closing the valve
the magic of disappearing something
that's the worth of the magician's hat
—something

How much should circulate
between the wall and the bookshelf
they're spaces
for mystery. It accumulates
regardless of quantity. It also leaves
room for escape
the concept of possibility helps
ward off claustrophobia

Sin romanticismo

Un solo grano de arena basta
entre el ojo y el párpado para que
moleste con pinchazos aun con el ojo
cerrado, inmóvil. Un solo grano de arena
para secar el agua; el ojo, seco, busca
llorar pero el dolor no es garantía
de lágrimas, el dolor no es
líquido de a gotas me echo
en los ojos el gesto de llorar
lo arrebatan las manos
que limpian rastros en los cachetes
como un ensayo general sin primera función
dolor que no se vuelca y sigue
secando de a pinchazos irritando la metáfora
del mar de lágrimas cuando se sabe que
el dolor se entiende
en el desierto.

No Romanticizing

A single grain of sand between
the eye and the eyelid is enough
to cause discomfort even with the eye
closed, motionless. A single grain of sand
can dry up the moisture; the dry eye tries
to cry but pain doesn't guarantee
tears, pain is not liquid
I put drops in
my eyes; my hands erase
the signs of weeping
clean up the traces on my cheeks
like a dress rehearsal with no premiere
the pain doesn't overflow but keeps on
drying needling irritating the metaphor
of the sea of tears when everyone knows that
grief makes sense
in the desert.

Tentáculos

El abrazo del aguaviva de febrero es el único
en 243 días contados. Los brazos de un ábaco
se mantienen paralelos. Es más fácil calificar
en colores los días pasados se resumen
las horas de ir a recalcar que malagua no
es adecuado para alguien que da
un contacto tan íntimo, arde
la huella del encuentro
en los brazos y las piernas la arena
me aleja el mar vivo.

Tentacles

The jellyfish in February gave me my only embrace
in 243 days straight. The arms of an abacus
stay parallel. It's easier to count
the days that have passed in colors
the number of hours shows that jellyfish is not
adequate to describe someone who offers
such intimate contact, the sand
soothes my arms and legs branded
by that encounter
the living sea shuns me.

Salvo los huecos

Irse cargando
en la valija algunos años con
huecos de gruyere

para poder remangarse
la camisa en días de calor

ver en el hueco un respiro
otro hueco otro respiro
la única posibilidad de estar

el queso marca
el tiempo y el gruyere
evita el refilón

Except for the Holes

Walk around lugging
a suitcase that holds a few years
full of holes like Gruyere

so you can roll up
your sleeves on hot days

see each hole as a breathing space
another hole another pause
the only way to be

cheese marks time
and Gruyere
makes that obvious

Los números

Todo puede empezar por un número. Por más raro que suene, un número puede hacer chispa. Yo que me aferraba a las letras para contar, ahora veo un número para narrar.

Numbers

It all may start with a number. This might sound odd, but a number can strike a spark. I who always clung to letters for recounting, now see a number tells a story.

About the Author

Laura Cesarco Eglin (Montevideo, Uruguay, 1976) is the author of three collections of poetry, *Calling Water by Its Name*, translated by Scott Spanbauer (Mouthfeel Press, 2016), *Sastrería* (Yaugurú, 2011), and *Los brazos del saguaro* (Yaugurú, 2015). A selection of poems from *Sastrería* was translated collaboratively into English with Teresa Williams, and subsequently published as the chapbook *Tailor Shop: Threads* (Finishing Line Press, 2013). Cesarco Eglin has also published the chapbook *Occasions to Call Miracles Appropriate* (The Lune, 2015). Her poems, as well as her translations (from the Spanish, Portuguese, Portuñol, and Galician), have appeared or are forthcoming in a variety of journals, including *Modern Poetry in Translation*, *eleven eleven*, *Puerto del Sol*, *Copper Nickel*, *Spoon River Poetry Review*, *Arsenic Lobster*, *International Poetry Review*, *Tupelo Quarterly*, *Columbia Poetry Review*, *Virga*, *Blood Orange Review*, *Timber*, *Pretty Owl Poetry*, *Pilgrimage*, *Periódico de Poesía*, and more. Her poems are also featured in the Uruguayan women's section of *Palabras Errantes*, *Plusamérica: Latin American Literature in Translation*. Cesarco Eglin is the translator of *Of Death. Minimal Odes* by the Brazilian author Hilda Hilst (co•im•press, 2018). She is the co-founding editor and publisher of Veliz Books.

About the Translators

Jesse Lee Kercheval is the author of fifteen books, including the poetry collection *America That Island Off the Coast of France* (Tupelo Press, 2019), winner of the Dorset Prize. Her translations include *The Invisible Bridge: Selected Poems of Circe Maia* (University of Pittsburgh Press, 2015) and *Fable of an Inconsolable Man* (Action Books, 2016) by Javier Etchevarren. She is the editor of *América invertida: An Anthology of Emerging Uruguayan Poets* (University of New Mexico Press, 2016). She was a 2016 NEA Fellow in Translation and is currently the Zona Gale Professor of English at the University of Wisconsin-Madison.

Catherine Jagoe is a poet, essayist, and ATA-certified translator with a PhD in Spanish literature from the University of Cambridge, England. In recent years, she has translated work by the contemporary Uruguayan poets Paula Simonetti, Luis Bravo, and Sebastián Rivero, some of which has appeared in *Tupelo Quarterly, American Poetry Review, Modern Poetry in Translation, Drunken Boat,* and in the anthology *América invertida.* She has also translated two novels, one from nineteenth-century Spain and the other twentieth-century Argentina. She holds a 2015 Pushcart Prize for creative nonfiction and three awards for her 2016 poetry book *Bloodroot.*

About the Artist

Juan Mastromatteo was born 1950 in Ischitella, Italy, but emigrated to Uruguay with his family when he was five. His works have appeared in more than seventy individual and group exhibitions in museums and cultural centers in Uruguay and abroad. His works are included in collections in Uruguay, Argentina, Brazil, Nicaragua, Spain, Germany, the United States and Canada.

"Raigambre" (oil on canvas, 0.60 x 0.70 meters, 2004) is part of a series where themes of life and death are combined with landscape and nature. The artist holds the reproduction rights.

About The Word Works

Since its founding in 1974, The Word Works has steadily published volumes of contemporary poetry and presented public programs. Its imprints include The Washington Prize, The Tenth Gate Prize, The Hilary Tham Capital Collection, and International Editions.

Monthly, The Word Works offers free literary programs in the Café Muse reading series at The Writers Center of Bethesda, MD, and each summer it holds free poetry programs in Washington, D.C.'s Rock Creek Park. Word Works programs have included "In the Shadow of the Capitol," a symposium and archival project on the African American intellectual community in segregated Washington, D.C.; the Gunston Arts Center Poetry Series; the Poet Editor panel discussions at The Writer's Center; Master Class workshops; and a writing retreat in Tuscany, Italy.

As a 501(c)3 organization, The Word Works has received awards from the National Endowment for the Arts, the National Endowment for the Humanities, the D.C. Commission on the Arts & Humanities, the Witter Bynner Foundation, Poets & Writers, The Writer's Center, Bell Atlantic, the David G. Taft Foundation, and others, including many generous private patrons.

An archive of artistic and administrative materials in the Washington Writing Archive housed in the George Washington University Gelman Library. It is a member of the Community of Literary Magazines and Presses and its books are distributed by Small Press Distribution.

wordworksbooks.org

Other Word Works Books

Annik Adey-Babinski, *Okay Cool No Smoking Love Pony*
Karren L. Alenier, *Wandering on the Outside*
Karren L. Alenier, ed., *Whose Woods These Are*
Karren L. Alenier & Miles David Moore, eds.,
    Winners: A Retrospective of the Washington Prize
Christopher Bursk, ed., *Cool Fire*
Willa Carroll, *Nerve Chorus*
Grace Cavalieri, *Creature Comforts*
Abby Chew, *A Bear Approaches from the Sky*
Nadia Colburn, *The High Shelf*
Barbara Goldberg, *Berta Broadfoot and Pepin the Short*
Akua Lezli Hope, *Them Gone*
Frannie Lindsay, *If Mercy*
Elaine Maggarrell, *The Madness of Chefs*
Marilyn McCabe, *Glass Factory*
Kevin McLellan, *Ornitheology*
JoAnne McFarland, *Identifying the Body*
Leslie McGrath, *Feminists Are Passing from Our Lives*
Ann Pelletier, *Letter That Never*
Ayaz Pirani, *Happy You Are Here*
W.T. Pfefferle, *My Coolest Shirt*
Jacklyn Potter, Dwaine Rieves, Gary Stein, eds.,
    Cabin Fever: Poets at Joaquin Miller's Cabin
Robert Sargent, *Aspects of a Southern Story*
    & *A Woman from Memphis*
Miles Waggener, *Superstition Freeway*
Fritz Ward, *Tsunami Diorama*
Camille-Yvette Welsch, *The Four Ugliest Children in Christendom*
Amber West, *Hen & God*
Maceo Whitaker, *Narco Farm*
Nancy White, ed., *Word for Word*

INTERNATIONAL EDITIONS BOOKS

Kajal Ahmad (Alana Marie Levinson-LaBrosse, Mewan Nahro Said Sofi, and Darya Abdul-Karim Ali Najin, trans., with Barbara Goldberg), *Handful of Salt*
Keyne Cheshire (trans.), *Murder at Jagged Rock: A Tragedy by Sophocles*
Jeannette L. Clariond (Curtis Bauer, trans.), *Image of Absence*
Jean Cocteau (Mary-Sherman Willis, trans.), *Grace Notes*
Yoko Danno & James C. Hopkins, *The Blue Door*
Moshe Dor, Barbara Goldberg, Giora Leshem, eds., *The Stones Remember: Native Israeli Poets*
Moshe Dor (Barbara Goldberg, trans.), *Scorched by the Sun*
Vladimir Levchev (Henry Taylor, trans.), *Black Book of the Endangered Species*

THE TENTH GATE PRIZE

Jennifer Barber, *Works on Paper*, 2015
Lisa Lewis, *Taxonomy of the Missing*, 2017
Brad Richard, *Parasite Kingdom*, 2018
Roger Sedarat, *Haji As Puppet*, 2016
Lisa Sewell, *Impossible Object*, 2014

THE WASHINGTON PRIZE

Nathalie Anderson, *Following Fred Astaire*, 1998
Michael Atkinson, *One Hundred Children Waiting for a Train*, 2001
Molly Bashaw, *The Whole Field Still Moving Inside It*, 2013
Carrie Bennett, *biography of water*, 2004
Peter Blair, *Last Heat*, 1999
John Bradley, *Love-in-Idleness: The Poetry of Roberto Zingarello*, 1995, 2ND edition 2014
Christopher Bursk, *The Way Water Rubs Stone*, 1988
Richard Carr, *Ace*, 2008
Jamison Crabtree, *Rel[AM]ent*, 2014
Jessica Cuello, *Hunt*, 2016
Barbara Duffey, *Simple Machines*, 2015
B. K. Fischer, *St. Rage's Vault*, 2012
Linda Lee Harper, *Toward Desire*, 1995
Ann Rae Jonas, *A Diamond Is Hard But Not Tough*, 1997
Susan Lewis, *Zoom*, 2017
Frannie Lindsay, *Mayweed*, 2009
Richard Lyons, *Fleur Carnivore*, 2005
Elaine Magarrell, *Blameless Lives*, 1991
Fred Marchant, *Tipping Point*, 1993, 2ND edition 2013
Nils Michals, *Gembox*
Ron Mohring, *Survivable World*, 2003
Barbara Moore, *Farewell to the Body*, 1990
Brad Richard, *Motion Studies*, 2010
Jay Rogoff, *The Cutoff*, 1994
Prartho Sereno, *Call from Paris*, 2007, 2ND edition 2013
Enid Shomer, *Stalking the Florida Panther*, 1987
John Surowiecki, *The Hat City After Men Stopped Wearing Hats*, 2006
Miles Waggener, *Phoenix Suites*, 2002
Charlotte Warren, *Gandhi's Lap*, 2000
Mike White, *How to Make a Bird with Two Hands*, 2011
Nancy White, *Sun, Moon, Salt*, 1992, 2ND edition 2010
George Young, *Spinoza's Mouse*, 1996

THE HILARY THAM CAPITAL COLLECTION

Nathalie Anderson, *Stain*
Mel Belin, *Flesh That Was Chrysalis*
Carrie Bennett, *The Land Is a Painted Thing*
Doris Brody, *Judging the Distance*
Sarah Browning, *Whiskey in the Garden of Eden*
Grace Cavalieri, *Pinecrest Rest Haven*
Cheryl Clarke, *By My Precise Haircut*
Christopher Conlon, *Gilbert and Garbo in Love*
    & *Mary Falls: Requiem for Mrs. Surratt*
Donna Denizé, *Broken Like Job*
W. Perry Epes, *Nothing Happened*
David Eye, *Seed*
Bernadette Geyer, *The Scabbard of Her Throat*
Elizabeth Gross, *this body / that lightning show*
Barbara G. S. Hagerty, *Twinzilla*
Lisa Hase-Jackson, *Flint & Fire*
James Hopkins, *Eight Pale Women*
Donald Illich, *Chance Bodies*
Brandon Johnson, *Love's Skin*
Thomas March, *Aftermath*
Marilyn McCabe, *Perpetual Motion*
Judith McCombs, *The Habit of Fire*
James McEwen, *Snake Country*
Miles David Moore, *The Bears of Paris* & *Rollercoaster*
Kathi Morrison-Taylor, *By the Nest*
Tera Vale Ragan, *Reading the Ground*
Michael Shaffner, *The Good Opinion of Squirrels*
Maria Terrone, *The Bodies We Were Loaned*
Hilary Tham, *Bad Names for Women* & *Counting*
Barbara Ungar, *Charlotte Brontë, You Ruined My Life* & *Immortal Medusa*
Jonathan Vaile, *Blue Cowboy*
Rosemary Winslow, *Green Bodies*
Michele Wolf, *Immersion*
Joe Zealberg, *Covalence*

www.ingramcontent.com/pod-product-compliance
Lightning Source LLC
Chambersburg PA
CBHW020857160426

43192CB00007B/959